Pages Called Holy

Pages Called Holy

Poems

J. TED VOIGT

RESOURCE *Publications* · Eugene, Oregon

PAGES CALLED HOLY
Poems

Resource Publications
A Division of Wipf and Stock Publishers
199 W. 8th Ave., Suite 3
Eugene, OR 97401

www.wipfandstock.com

ISBN 13: 978-1-60608-742-8

Manufactured in the U.S.A.

To my wife, Sarah, *mi vida, te amo*

Contents

VI

I

THESE PAGES CALLED HOLY

I don't understand it
(I'll do it
but I don't understand it)
because you asked me
even though it doesn't really make sense to me
I will lay down my logic
a sacrifice of sense
because you asked me to
and because I believe

there is more than words
on these pages before me
these pages called Holy

there is more than words
in these prayers I utter
and there is more than silence
in the response I hear.

I will remove the scaffolding around my mind
mental structures deconstructed
on the altar

This is my reasonable act of worship:
I offer my reason
a sacrifice Holy and acceptable.

A FIRM FOUNDATION

Give me something to stand on
give me solid ground
and I will build my life on it

Show me truth
and I will put my trust in it

Don't tell me to stand on the Rock
and then spend 20 minutes
pelting me with puny pebbles

What is sand but tiny
pieces of rock

individually solid
collectively weak for
foundation building

LANGUAGE BARRIER

. . . yes it is as you say . . .
The words you speak are true
everything you say is true
it must be true
I read it on the internet
I saw it on TV
I read it in my Bible
The text, a source
like an ancient newspaper
written in holineese
but I only speak earthish
I need a translation
not a paraphrase
not a literal take
just a translation
let my life be scripture
translated into the language
of the lives of lost people
but then I would have to go out
leave this place
the place where you said I needed to be
. . . it is you who says it . . .

THE BEGINNING

i

I spent my afternoon
walking around the quaint
downtown of North Kansas City
eating cookies and falling in love
with poetry
My faithful friend Clive
needed a blood transfusion
(and his tires rotated)
and I suddenly had four free hours
alone
searching for a life blood of my own
and the *Republic of Poetry*

ii

I sat awake in bed
full of the energy
of poetry and coffee
I don't speak this language
but still I feel like a native
I belong to the republic
but I'm still learning the local dialect
no better way to understand
then to read the words he wrote
in the language he wrote them

iii

My Bible sits open on my lap
I belong to this country
but I pretend to be a citizen
of Earth
of these United States
I read the words on the page
but to read the true words
I need to learn the language
the language of love
the language of God
Justice and Peace.

II

TRANSLATION

What if creativity doesn't exist?
and all that is created
already existed
and all we do
as artists
musicians
poets
is see the beauty of what is
and translate it
into art
song
verse.

It is our nature
because before the beginning
God saw what existed in God
and translated God
into matter
earth, water, flesh
created not from nothing
but from the actual substance of God

What we need are more schools of language
to teach people to read the script
to hear the unique dialect
of the ancient language that is God
to train followers to listen
with much patience
as the words are often slow and hard to hear
though sometimes they come in a quick,
    quiet whisper
many words, fast but soft.
other times it may take years
to finish hearing a single word
monks
and seminarians
devote years, lifetimes,
to the careful study of
the grammar and punctuation
of God.
The vocabulary is peace and justice
and our work is that of
translators.

WORDS

Words are all we have
words will never be enough
but they're all we have

God
is a word we use
to describe the love we feel
not a person
not an idea
not a doctrine
God is love
concentrated
searingly strong
stinging and bleaching and warping
    all it touches
how dare you dilute it!
giving the people
white grape pomegranate juice
fresh baked white bread
false teaching
of false gods who
look
just
like
you.

THE IMAGE OF 3 GODS

i

In the mountains of east Tennessee
in an old farm house in the woods
a potter fills his front porch
with beautifully glazed ceramics
after dark
the pots can be heard
whispering about the potter
The Potter is the greatest of Pots
they say
It has infinite capacity, it is never full
It is flawless, without a single crack
and it's glaze is a brilliant rainbow of colors
Sometimes in the cold of winter
the pots have great arguments
about the shape of the Potter
and whether or not the Potter
has a handle

ii

In the bottom drawer
of an old metal cabinet
is a collection of Polaroids
snapped by a great Photographer
sometimes late at night

the Polaroids tell stories
about their brief encounters
with the Photographer and it's friends
The Photographer the greatest of Polaroids
infinitely flat, shiny, and unfaded by time
It's edges, they say, are unbendable
with corners more crisp then the day
        they were created
And sometimes the Polaroids are taken
        from the drawer
and carefully shown to others.
And when they return, they tell great stories
of the love and kindness and beautiful
        subject matter
of the Great Photographer.

iii
In churches across America
around the world
across the enlightenment
people are known to gather
and tell stories of the great Father
his arms hold me tight
they say
his heart breaks when I sin
and sometimes
they draw pictures

and they sing songs of the great person
the giant, almighty human
their creator.

PARADOX

A dynamic and ever changing God
who is eternal and never changes.
A people who have been taught for years
and now are finally beginning to realize
they know absolutely nothing.
Moving out from under the tyranny of dichotomy
into the present age of the reign of paradox,
for the first time ever what is said actually
     makes sense.
From inside simple, temporal, human skulls
looking beyond all that is seen to a God who is
     ever-present
thinking
Wow. God must really love paradox.

The permission to live in the mystery of God
could save the world a lot of hurt.

EROSION

A stone

sits exposed on the side of a mountain.

wind blows

rain falls

erosion is the only enemy

of our heroic stone

A stone is powerless to resist the forces of nature

in the wilderness

A stone collector

with an attic full of rocks

gathers the stone

and preserves him

salvation

REAL FEAR

Am I scared of God?

Is God real to me?

or do I just pretend?

Do I experience God?

or am I afraid of what I'll see?

If God were real

would I pray?

Do I pray now?
pray like there's someone listening?
Who am I talking to
when I pray
I am scared of someone
So I pray to no one
but no one isn't listening

HAIKU 001

the beauty of words
flowers. breezes. butterflies.
a nail piercing flesh.

III

ESCAPE

The season of revolution is here
cool wind blows through windows
recently opened for the first time in
what seems like ages.

Each day the sun gives summer
a new advantage, and at night
it retreats, regrouping
for the next day's battle.

A pool laps outside my window
still green and unswimable
but my clothes are filled with smoky hope
from the year's first cook-out

I force myself through prose
of South American uprisings
but each page brings only longing
for a cause of my own.

An armchair insurgency
is being fiercely imagined all around me
Shakespearian actors passionately dueling
to Shakespearian deaths.

I plot my escape.

ELEGY FOR ANTIOCH MALL

Last night I went walking
with the Ghost
of the American economy
while the thinkers debate whether or not
it's really dead.
sheets blowing in the unheated wind
cover the places where shoppers
once practiced their art.
The food court now reduced
to a short row of vending machines
happily displayed sodas
to a homeless man.
Only a few stubborn stores remain
obstinately advertising huge discounts
hoping the walkers
like me
might like a new, half price coat

for the

long

cold

night ahead.

SEPTEMBER 25TH

Today the wind is full of cautious joy.
A gust through my window
smirks as if to say "nothing this good
will last for long"
and we are free
at last from the oppression of humidity
and the captivity of wearing short pants.
today we are free, but we know that all too soon
our liberators will appoint a new government
and filled with their seasonal power we are
brought under a
new oppressor
and we wait for spring to free us again.
and we leave our shorts in the bottom drawer
        just in case.

HISTORY

The roots of history grow deep in time
and I am stuck in today
unable to see into the past lives earth

There are stories
growing up from the soil of human experience
and still I am stuck
unable to discern truth from fact

I am told of a God
the one who created
and then the sun comes up
and I am again stuck
trying to imagine the one who
lit the fire
in the eastern sky.

SANCTIFICATION

All I can do is ask

not work
not earn
not worry

just wait

waiting I thought would take forever

but before I think

forever

it's here

Peace I thought was gone

a sunken ship

a rotting corpse

like a crashing wave from nowhere

on a word written in sand

the hand of God nailed down

WAKE UP

WAKE UP

give me the words

come and listen

fuel my passion

speak loudly

listen without blinking your ears

teach my tongue

drink and live life

the words I don't know

abundantly- a surplus

words that give life

get out of your coma

words that

WAKE UP

THOUGHTS ON DUALITY AND IDENTITY IN THREE MOVEMENTS

i

What am I, a piece

of lumber?

a burlap sack of soy beans?

What crop am I

that you should

harvest me?

gather me into your barns

ship me to your supermarkets

ii

And on what shelf

do I belong?

I can´t see beneath this

thin, aluminum skin

and my label fell off

let´s start a revolution

you take yours off too

no longer shall we be judged

By the colorful wrappers
adorning us!
No longer shall our contents be
passed over carelessly
by people who hate lima beans
or those mildly allergic to carrots.

iii

What am I
a lump of meat?
and a cosmic ball of psychic energy?
Am I one, or pieces
and if pieces how many?
Mind, Body, Soul, Spirit?
Will death
like some portly butcher
divide me with his cleaver
soul from body
one to rot
the other finally free?

HOW TO . . .

. . . Be Someone:

Get Degree(s)

Start Blog

Attend Conferences

Write Non Fiction

Go on a book tour

Lead Workshop at said conference

Guest write for another blog more popular
   than yours

Find someone to mentor

Start a Nonprofit company

Appoint yourself President of said company

. . . Do Something:

Find something you love

Start doing it

Don't stop

Don't move

Find someone you love and do it with them

Find a mentor

Keep doing it

Find out you've been doing it wrong,
   start doing it right

Don't tell anyone you're doing it

Have kids, teach them to do it

IV

ECONOMICS OF PRAYER

In the economy of prayer
requests are exchanged
a commerce of illness and loss
a banker in a robe and stole
hopes to show us the cost of salvation
of healing
of redemption
citizens of the kingdom make their deposits
I make a withdrawal
(an escape really)
I'm selling off my stock
and investing in something else
I'm sure to lose it all
I am ready to lose it all.
This prayer has no pay off
just simple, selfless obedience
this then, is how you should pray

THE STRUGGLE

She just can't believe.
She can't believe there is a God
who made her poor.
She can't believe God
doesn't want her eight children
to eat tonight.
She can't believe. she won't.
As she looks back on her life
full of broken years
she just can't believe.
She can't believe there exists someone
somewhere
something
who is at the same time
all-powerful
and all-loving
because she has no power
and she has never felt loved
and so she can't believe, she won't.
it would be far too painful to believe.
But she has to believe
she must, she needs to believe
to get through the day
she has to believe that

the future of her eight kids
isn't hanging on her ability to provide
she has to believe because
she knows she can't do it alone
she has to believe
she must
she has to believe that
in each tough break is grace
that each good thing is a blessing
and that there is a reason to hope
for things to get better
she has to believe
she must, she needs to believe
it would be far too painful not to believe.

A THEOLOGY OF PAIN

Belief is forged in deepest pain
to deny one's belief
is to deny the flames
ever burned

An innocent victim murdered
An innocent man convicted

A child lost in a terrorist attack
A child lost in the resulting war

A devastating miscarriage
A devastating rape and pregnancy

A life of captivity to addiction
A life of captivity to religion

ever burning
to deny the flames
is to deny belief
forged in deepest pain

DELETE

I am surrounded with knowledge
stacked 5 rows high
and little else but the silence
that seems somehow connected to knowledge
as if directly related by some forgotten
principle of physics
$K = 2 S / P$
where the amount of Knowledge
is equal to twice the amount of Silence
divided by the number of People in the
close vicinity

And people who spend a lot of time alone
in the still and quiet seclusion
of a car with no radio
must also be the wise sages of our generation
it must be hard to disappear
when you're surrounded with eyes
that connect to other eyes
that see through all the noise
delete
is one of the most powerful words we know
there is nothing
that is quite as gone as something deleted.
simplicity is not found when everything is gone
it's found when everything is gone except
 one thing
because when everything is gone
nothing remains
and if you've ever known nothingness
it's not easy
it's not peaceful
it's not simple.
I leave this temple
break my radio
delete my hard drive
add one.

ONE

It's getting harder to believe
Believe with your entire being
Belief like a lifestyle
not just a costume
it's a skin color
we're moving backwards
through civil rights
to apartheid
you can believe anything
as long as you believe everything
how is it logical to believe in one
when you could believe in many?
One is not as lonely
as it used to be.

BELIEVE/IMAGINE

Belief is an incredibly difficult concept for me
    to understand.
In fact the more I think about it the more
    complicated it seems.
Ask a Christian what someone needs to do to get
    to heaven, and with some variation the
basic answer you {should} get is "Believe in Jesus."

But what does it mean to believe in him?

Believe he exists?

even the demons believe, and shudder

No it must mean something else.

To have belief we must first have unknown

To know everything is to believe nothing

though still it seems the more we learn, the

 greater mystery God becomes

and the greater the mystery,

 the more we need belief.

And the more we need belief, the more we strive

 for it.

And the more we strive for belief, the more likely

 we are to find God.

Believing isn't something that happens in

 a moment-

It can't be impelled or ignited or inspired

Belief takes practice and patience and persistence

it is so much harder to believe

then the average American churchgoer would

 have you think.

In fact I think most people don't believe in God.

C.S. Lewis says

God is ultimately Superior

and if we don't know ourselves to be ultimately

 inferior to God

we don't know God
we must not believe in the true God
we believe in an imaginary God
we imagine God.
so should we go on imaging God?
Pursuing an imagined God?
Worshiping the God we imagine in?
How long will you imagine in God?

I don´t imagine in God the father almighty
Creator of heaven and earth
and in his only son our Lord Jesus Christ
Who was conceived by the Holy Spirit
born of the Virgin Mary
Suffered under Pontius Pilate
Was crucified, dead and buried
he descended in Hell
and the third day I don´t imagine he rose again
    from the dead
and ascended into heaven
where he sits at the right hand of God the father
    almighty
from there he will come to judge the living
    and the dead
I don´t imagine in the Holy Spirit
the holy catholic church
the communion of saints

the forgiveness of sins

the resurrection of the body

and the life everlasting amen.

no.

I can't imagine any more.

I can't imagine a God who hates science.

Who favors the death penalty, but hates gays
and unwed mothers.

I can't imagine a God who blesses America and
watches Africa suffer with AIDS and malaria.

I can't imagine a God who wants war, or bombs
or guns or secret prisons.

I won't imagine in this God; there's a real God
out there.

I want to believe in a God who is bigger.

A God who is like creation.

A God who loves like a dying man.

A God like a cloud

and a flame

and a river

and a tree

and a human

and like nothing I have ever imagined before

The God I believe in

I can't even imagine.

V

MISSIONAL DECONSTRUCTION

we gotta grow the church

we need to educate
because we gotta grow the church

we need good leaders
who can educate
because we gotta grow the church

we need good youth groups
to make good leaders
who can educate
because we gotta grow the church

we need exciting youth leaders
because we need big youth groups
to make lots of good leaders
who can educate
because we gotta grown the church

we need a summer mission trip
because that's what exciting youth leaders do
to make big youth groups
to attract good leaders
who can educate
because we gotta grow the church

A good church has lots of people
who show up for lots of events
and do lots of Bible Studies
who can talk about the Bible
who can share their faith
who can care about people
the way God does.

Well actually
A good church just has lots of events
and people who do Bible studies
and can talk about the Bible
and share their faith
and care about people
the way God does.

But really
A good church focuses on Bible Study
so people can talk about the Bible
so they can share their faith

and care about people
the way God does.

So then actually
a good church has people who talk about
     the Bible
and share their faith
and care about people
the way God does?

But what if a good church
just shares their faith
and cares about people
the way God does?

I believe a good church
cares about people
the way God does.

SOME EASTER THOUGHTS

Those who die are dead
they are buried and decay
and this tomb stands open wide
there is no body rotting
impossibly true, the dead live

Easter is not just today
not just this story
it's not just about us
and God
it's about love
about relationships
and justice and mystery.
This morning we woke up
gathered with the Faithful of the Lord
and the not so faithful
we celebrated our faith
talked about our pain
we ate together
and for one day
we were the Church

MO(U)RNING WORSHIP

You Pharisees
with your selections of scripture
like rancid sirloin
you've butchered my Word
I weep for you

You Pharisees
with your ammunition

shooting each other
putting holes in my Church
I weep for you

You Pharisees
with your Sunday morning show
the monologue, the musical guest
you've cheapened worship
I weep for you

STOP

Stop attending church.
PLEASE
We cannot take much more of this
Stop attending church
before everything falls apart
attendance
complacent
ambivalent
attendance
is not
of the Kingdom of God
We don't attend
the Kingdom of God
its not a secret society

or a fraternal order
or a club or a team or a band
it's a Way
it's THE Way
the way is here
and the time is right
trade attendance for existence
stop going to church
and start being the Church.

OTRO MUNDO ES POSIBLE

Scientists, with their telescopes gaze
into the heavens, searching for other worlds
and here we sit
in coffee shops and libraries
talking about the ways
another world is possible
on earth.
Poised like explorers
pilgrims
setting out to discover the new world
we're back at Plymouth rock
except this time it's not religious freedom
but freedom from religion

which we are seeking
and we will not yield.

SPRINGTIME FOR A CHURCH

The ground beneath our church is frozen
it can only be melted
by the tears of the proud.
Only when liberals and conservatives embrace
will the icy soil of our foundation
turn again to clay.
When women step up to the pulpit
and men to the front of the Sunday school room
and the children worship with grown-ups
shaking geothermal maracas and tambourines
    loudly
When the elders
in their musty board room
stop trying to please people
and start trying to please God
then new life emerges
from thawed, healed earth.

THE NIGHT THE CHURCH CAUGHT FIRE

What if your church was on fire?
Would you be afraid?
Or would you cheer on as tongues
singed and purified?
Would you pour water on the flames?
Or would you call your neighbors
for a cook out
stoke the fire
and enjoy the warmth
of community?
And when at last the burning ceases
would you rebuild?
Get out the old blue prints
and start reconstructing?
Would you go on living in the
charred shell of what used to be?
Or would you start new?
Go out in search of new ways
new celebrations
of the night the church caught fire?

ORDER OF THE BROKEN HEARTED

We are a Holy Order
of the brokenhearted
unreasonably in love
with sinners
nauseated by the thought of sin
hopeful-ly in love with the poor
counting ourselves among them
we strive to help even when we can´t help
as we lack visible, tangible, credible resources
we meet violence with peace
knowing this is
sometimes
how martyrs are made.
Our call to holiness
is a call to broken heartedness
The One who calls us
is The One who heals us
our creed is The Spirit
The Spirit is our only hope
and we are a hopeful
joyful
brokenhearted
brethren

VI

A LEAK

Your isms are leaking.
It's getting all over your faith.
Your consumerism
individualism
capitalism
they're leaking into your religious life
leaving stains on your belief.
Your isms are leaking all over the place.

ERUPTION

A thin man with thick black rim glasses
slowly stands up in front of a room full of
people.
He pauses for a moment in thought,
and then calmly begins to tell me
that my religion is on fire.

And that it's a good thing.

We are the spiritual fire-walkers
If we stand still for too long our feet will get
stuck in cooling lava
and we are still trying not to change.

EXPORTATION

Religion is poured into burlap sacks
loaded into gray hulled ships
in gritty ports across North America.
A southern town on the eastern seaboard
remembers a time when it was tobacco or sugar
and weeps.
Meanwhile farmers across the Midwest are
hauling in the crops on Sunday morning
developing strategies for the sowing of seeds
and targeting targets
the hunters and gatherers
of the new American commodity.

GOOD NEWS FOR THE
MODERN MAN

In a dark urban corner of America
A man stands on a street corner

and practices his art.
more than art
It's a calling
sometimes happily answered
A gift he never asked for.
A life he chooses every day
but never would have chosen for himself.
Each day unsuspecting pedestrians
sustain head on collisions
at the intersection of Main Street
and Church Avenue.
They never realized that anything was wrong
but such are the ways of belief accidents
We don't ask for our beliefs
but still they find us
when we're not looking.

THE EVANGELIST

6:15 AM
The Evangelist
gets up early this morning
spending time with his prayer list
and his 365 page booklet
of comfort and joy.

His crisp khaki pants
and short sleeve button up shirt
freshly ironed
he is ready for the day.
Strapping on his utility belt
he feels like a cross between batman
and John the Baptist
rejected by his society
working thanklessly to save people.
But with the batmobile in the shop
he´s on foot today.
In the summertime he wears no socks
between his loafers
and his beautiful feet
which he pedicures in accordance with
Isaiah 52:7
and he´s on his way

9:23 AM
8 blocks to his first stop
a burden which the evangelist gladly endures
he enters the coffee shop
scoping out potential targets
it´s busy, for a Wednesday morning
he finds a seat
on the far side of the room
from the group of men who appear to be

already converted.
he sets his bible next to his double mocha
and begins to feel the spirit work
About three sips in he is approached by a man
who prepares to present the gospel powerfully
    and relevantly
he is asked if anyone is using this chair.

11:03
The evangelist hits the street
having found no opportunities to share
over coffee
and prayer-walks until lunch.
rounding the corner
he pictures himself
the urban spiritual cowboy
his belt carries two holsters
on his left, the mighty blackberry
with video capabilities
and I video version of the gospel preloaded.
on his right, what appears to be another
    cell phone
with sharp square edges
and glossy colored surfaces.
Finally, just before heading home
he sees someone
a man, disheveled, sitting on the sidewalk

with nothing better to do
the evangelist approaches
makes casual conversation
he starts with the weather
moves skillfully to the heat
then subtly to flames of a more
eternal nature.
he reaches to his right holster
and draws a set of 8 colored cubes
his fingers nimbly folding the interconnected
    blocks
pictures appear, vanish
a story unfolds
a crack
a cross
a stone
a man
a bridge
the man responds politely but uninterested

12:21

the evangelist leaves some carefully selected
    literature
with the man
and heads to the bat cave to eat.
slightly disappointed at the opportunities of
    the morning

but reminding himself it was all worthwhile
if he was able to convert
just one lost soul.

MY MANIFESTO

Talk less
hear more and listen
Spend less
save more and give
Ask less
offer more and work
Move less
be still and rest
Know less
learn more and think
Create less
Feel more and translate

ELEGY FOR THE MODERN

You'll have to forgive me
if I seem skeptical
of your government
your empire
your idolatrous patriotism.

Your flag waving
is distracting me
Your insistence on logic
and rationality
as if thinking is the way
to God
to Heaven
to Salvation
I reject your modern thought
your enlightenment has darkened this world
Evil
is a result of logic
and can be eliminated
if we could just stop thinking
and start loving

REFLECTING ON A JOURNEY

Studies have shown:
too much of something is bad for your health
Toxins build up
clogging things
making your cells go insane
and self destruct.
And I take myself too seriously.

My soul has cancer

from too much pride and

ambition.

For 10 years I have been taught that with

enough work I can fix myself

for 20 years

I have been broken

Now only now as I watch

self destruction all around me

Can I see that the only way to stop

gathering toxins

is to

just

stop.

rest.

learn.

learning is good for the soul, not because you

gain knowledge

but rather because you discover how little

you know.

renuevame ser

lo que tu me has creido ser

And I am watching now

I am listening

I am pushing myself

from the inside out

in the direction from which I can
sometimes hear voices.
And I have heard them
There have been voices in my life
(in my head?)
Call my name
in undeniable ways.
And now the noises of life
have become so loud
bending, crunching, crumpling the voices
until I can no longer hear them
and wander away.
I have wandered to where I could not hear at all
and there all I could do
is trust my memory that
once there were voices
and then stop.
Begin the difficult work of slowly
removing
each
individual
sound
each wave
one by one, examining it
studying it
and upon realizing that it´s not the voice
silencing it

until as a carving emerges from stone
as a diamond is cut
as an orchestra tunes
beauty is all that remains
and I am finally left with just the voice
and nothing to do but follow.
For 10 years I have been taught
to follow what I feel is right
For 20 years I have followed devoutly
and only found that I am not to be trusted
Now I am ready to trust my life
to someone who can
do more with it than I can.
renuevame ser
lo que tu me has creido ser